Hymns and Spirituals
for Fingerstyle Guitar
by James Douglas Esmond

ISBN: 978-1-57424-230-0
SAN 683-8022

Cover guitar - J-90 Eagle Brazilian Rose 3
with thanks to Steve Helgeson, Moonstone Guitars

Cover by Design Associates

Copyright © 2008 CENTERSTREAM Publishing, LLC
P.O. Box 17878 - Anaheim Hills, CA 92817

www.centerstream-usa.com

Contents and CD Track List

Songs graded from 1-9, with playing tips

Wade In The Water - *Easy (1)*
This should be a pretty easy piece for most beginners. You can really go for as much connecting of the melody line as possible and there are many open strings used.

Amazing Grace (1ˢᵗ) - *Easy (2)*
With this piece, try to keep the fingers of the left hand down as long as possible between chord changes, especially in the second half, to ensure maximum legato. Also, de-emphasize any inner voices to bring out the melody.

Were You There...? (1ˢᵗ) - *Easy (3)*
Take at a pace slow enough but not too slow that the inner voices and bass line don't have connection.

Jesus Walked This Lonesome Valley (1ˢᵗ) - *Easy(3)*
This piece requires a very light touch with the left hand to ensure Legato. Don't be afraid to shorten chords such as the one on **beat 3 of measure 6** to ensure that the melodic flow does not get interrupted.

It's Me, It's Me O Lord, (Standing in the need of prayer) (1ˢᵗ) - *Easy (3)*
Be careful of the rhythms in this arrangement, there are a lot of syncopations. It is okay to be more articulate and play some things very staccato, such as the chords under the melody in **measure 1**.

Swing Low, Sweet Chariot (1ˢᵗ) -*Medium (4)*
This is primarily a two voice arrangement. The bass line should be brought out as much as possible without letting it overshadow the melody.

Every Time I Feel The Spirit - *Medium (4)*
This is a very energetic, upbeat arrangement and therefore the rhythm is of utmost importance. It can also be very articulated and somewhat more staccato in some places.

I've Got Peace Like A River - *Medium (5)*
Play as Legato as possible! Picking a slower tempo would work for this piece.

Steal Away To Jesus (1ˢᵗ) - *Medium (6)*
Take at a pace slow enough but not too slow that the inner voices and bass line don't have connection. Be careful of the hinge bar in **measure 2** and really try to stick to the fingerings given.

Swing Low, Sweet Chariot (2ⁿᵈ) -*Medium (6)*
Same as the first Swing Low (#6) but with more difficulty.

Lift Every Voice And Sing - *Medium (6)*
Stick to the fingerings given and this arrangement should play itself. Hold onto things in the left hand as long as possible to ensure Legato.

It's Me, It's Me O Lord, (Standing in the need of prayer) (2ⁿᵈ) - *Medium (6)*
Same as the first Standing in the need of Prayer (#5) but with more difficulty.

Down by The Riverside - *Medium (6)*
This is primarily a two voice arrangement. The bass line should be brought out as much as possible without letting it overshadow the melody.

Amazing Grace (2ⁿᵈ) - *Hard(7)*
Picking a slow enough tempo is very important for this version, mostly due to the continuous triplets. There are a fair amount of bars but they are all very necessary.

Jesus Walked This Lonesome Valley (2ⁿᵈ) - *Hard(7)*
Same as the first Standing in the need of Prayer (#4) but with much more difficulty and more inner voices. Take as slow as necessary to really connect everything.

Steal Away To Jesus (2ⁿᵈ) - *Hard (8)*
Same as the first Standing in the need of Prayer (#10) but with more difficulty a much harder middle section. All bars should be prepared very carefully.

Were You There...? (2ⁿᵈ) - *Hard (9)*
This is the most challenging of all the pieces both in length and technique necessary. Try to follow every fingering as well as you can.

Foreword

For as long as I have had musical opinions, I have always been fond of the Genre of the Spiritual. These songs have a raw energy that is so much greater than the sum of their notes and rhythms. I have often been moved by performances of spirituals in larger venues such as choirs, but it wasn't until recently that I discovered the intense impact of spirituals by a solo instrument. One night at a talent show for a music camp where I was teaching, a young woman who came to participate decided she would sing a medley of three spirituals; Wade in the Water, Amazing Grace and Sometimes I Feel Like a Motherless Child. In the midst of many other more elaborate performances featuring large groups of musicians, this woman simply sang unaccompanied, and although she embellished slightly, the overwhelming message was clear; spirituals have depth and soul that reaches right inside the heart of the listener, even when sung from a single voice on an otherwise empty stage. As she sang, it struck me how beautiful these songs could be on my instrument of choice, the Guitar, and it is now my pleasure to share my interpretations with you.

I tried to keep the arrangements as simple as possible, while retaining their original character. The second version of Amazing Grace(#16)is the only one in which I have embellished the melody. Feel free to add more or less repeats as well in any of these pieces, it is consistent with the style. I think you will find these pieces to be playable , yet challenging and fun. Have a good time.

James Douglas Esmond

Biography

James Douglas Esmond started playing the guitar seriously in his teens. He received his Bachelor's of Music Theory and Classical Guitar performance from Ithaca College, Ithaca, N.Y. Upon graduating he became involved in church music. He has held positions in various churches, as a guitarist, organist, singer and conductor. In addition to his church work, he also teaches privately and writes and arranges compositions in various genres and styles. He currently serves as the Organist/Music Coordinator at Newtonville Methodist Church in Loudonville, N.Y.

Wade In The Water

African American Spiritual, Arr. by J.Douglas Esmond

Amazing Grace

African American Spiritual, Arr. by J.Douglas Esmond

Peaceful,serene

♩=80

Were You There When They Crucified My Lord?

African American Spiritual, Arr. by J.Douglas Esmond

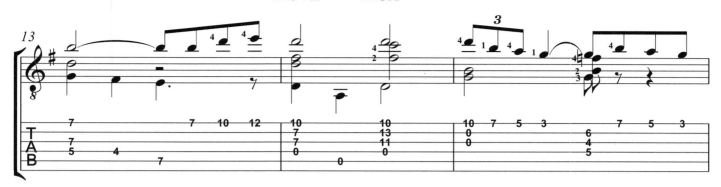

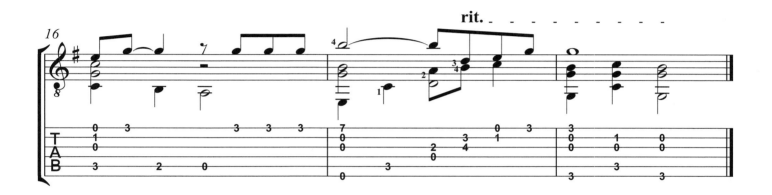

11

Jesus Walked This Lonesome Valley

African American Spiritual, Arr.by J.Douglas Esmond

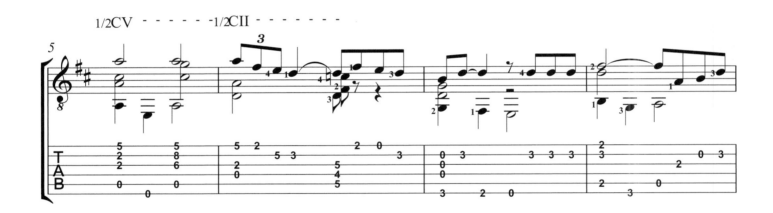

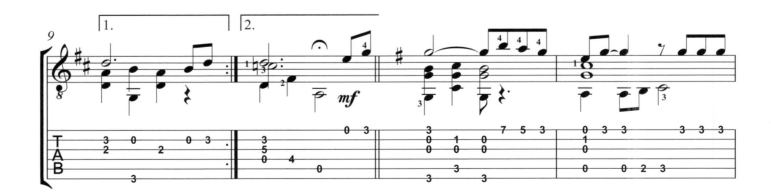

This arrangement copyright © Centerstream Publications, LLC

It's Me, It's Me, O Lord
(Standing in the need of Prayer)

African American Spiritual, Arr. by J.Douglas Esmond

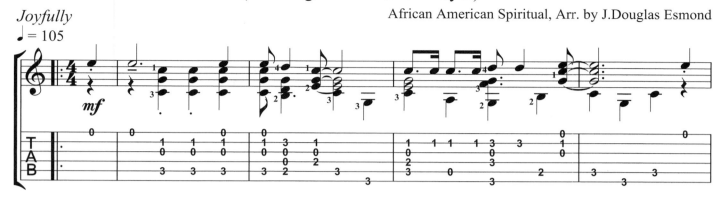

(3rd time)Fine

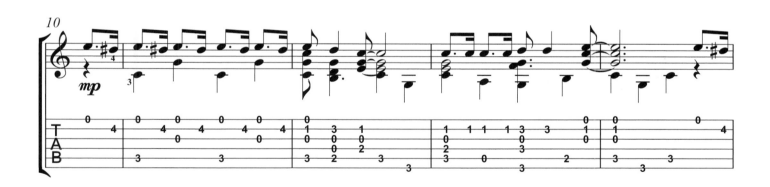

D.C.al fine

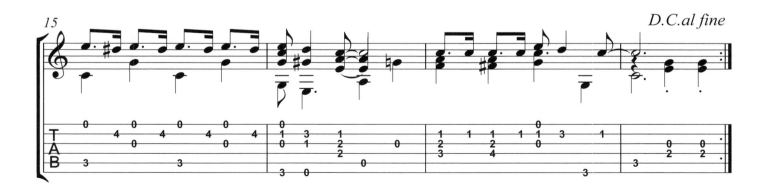

Swing Low, Sweet Chariot

African American Spiritual, Arr. by J.Douglas Esmond

Every Time I feel The Spirit
(Pentacost)

*Swing eighth notes

Joyfully

African American Spiritual, Arr. by J.Douglas Esmond

♩ = 110

I've Got Peace Like A River

African American Spiritual, Arr. by J. Douglas Esmond

Steal Away To Jesus

African American Spiritual, Arr. by J.Douglas Esmond

Swing Low, Sweet Chariot

African American Spiritual, Arr. by J.Douglas Esmond

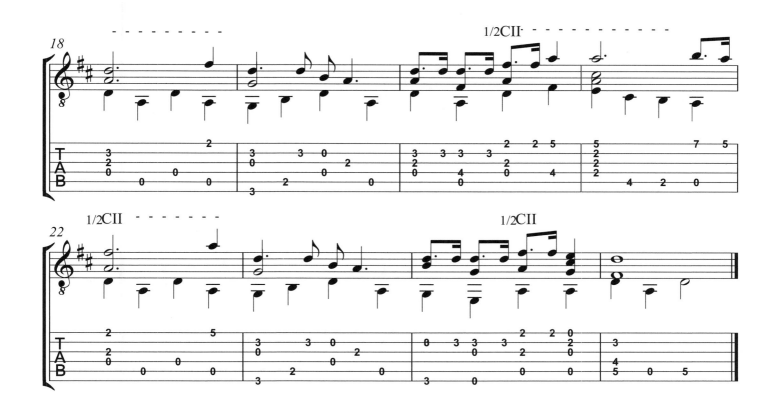

Lift Every Voice And Sing

African-American Spiritual, Arr. by J.Douglas Esmond

It's Me, It's Me, O Lord
(Standing in the need of Prayer)

African American Spiritual, Arr. by J.Douglas Esmond

Down By The Riverside
(Study war no more)

African American Spiritual, Arr. by J.Douglas Esmond

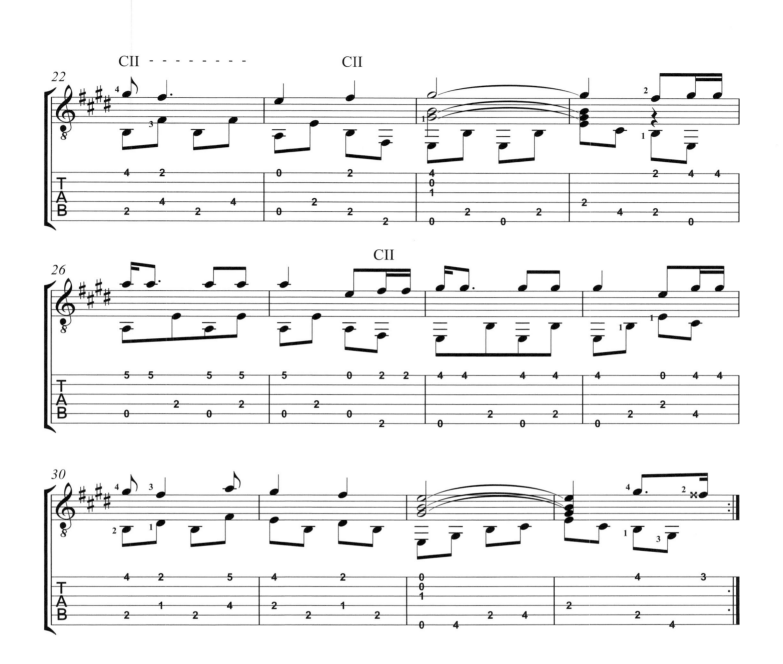

Amazing Grace

African American Spiritual, Arr. by J.Douglas Esmond

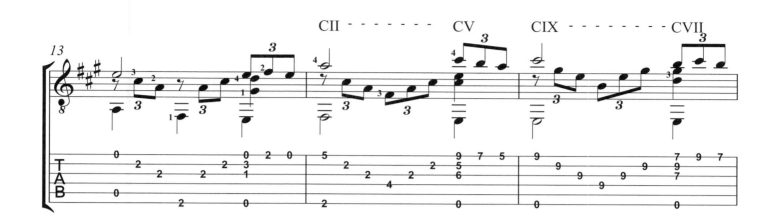

Jesus Walked This Lonesome Valley

African American Spiritual, Arr.by J.Douglas Esmond

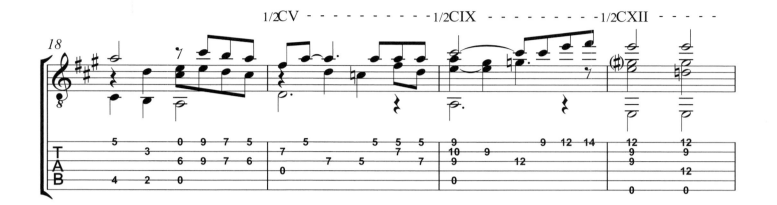

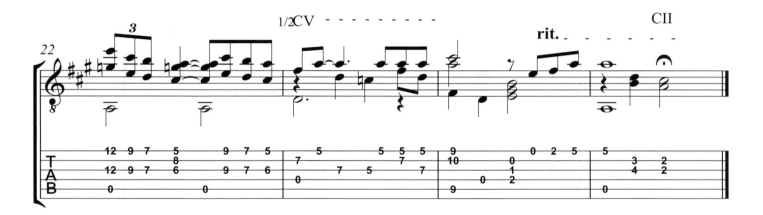

Steal Away To Jesus

African American Spiritual, Arr. by J.Douglas Esmond

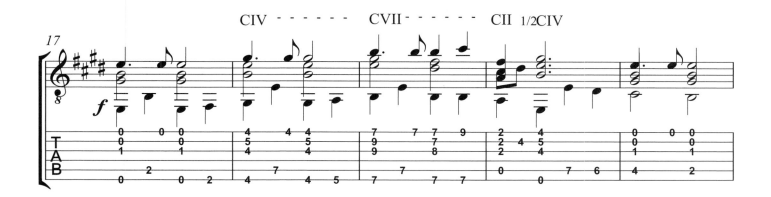

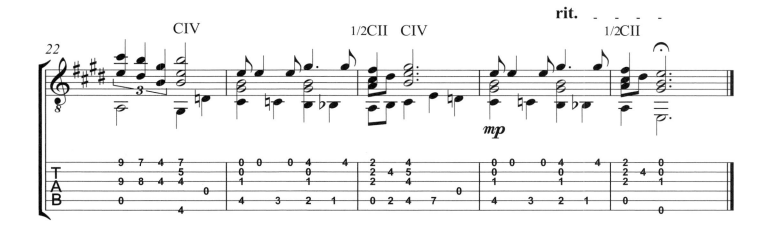

Were You There When They Crucified My Lord?

African American Spiritual, Arr. by J.Douglas Esmond

Lyrics

Amazing Grace

Amazing grace! How sweet the sound
That saved a wretch like me!
I once was lost, but now am found,
Was blind, but now I see.

'Twas grace that taught my heart to fear
And grace my fears relieved;
How precious did that grace appear
The hour I first believed!

Thro' many dangers, toils and snares,
I have already come;
'Tis grace hath brought me safe thus far,
And grace will lead me home.

Yea, when this flesh and heart shall fail,
And mortal life shall cease,
I shall possess within the veil
A life of joy and peace.

Swing Low, Sweet Chariot

Swing low, sweet chariot,
Coming for to carry me home
Swing low sweet chariot
Coming for to carry me home.

I looked over Jordan and what did I see?
Coming for to carry me home,
A band of angels coming after me,
Coming for to carry me home.

If you get there before I do,
Coming for to carry me home,
Tell all my friends I'm coming to,
Coming for to carry me home.

I'm sometimes up and sometimes down,
Coming for to carry me home,
But still my soul feels heavenly bound,
Coming for to carry me home.

Jesus Walked This Lonesome Valley

Jesus walked this lonesome valley.
He had to walk it by Himself;
O, nobody else could walk it for Him,
He had to walk it by Himself.

We must walk this lonesome valley,
We have to walk it by ourselves;
O, nobody else can walk it for us,
We have to walk it by ourselves.

You must go and stand your trial,
You have to stand it by yourself,
O, nobody else can stand it for you,
You have to stand it by yourself.

It's Me, It's Me O Lord

It's me, It's me O Lord,
An' I'm standin' in the need of prayer.
It's me, It's me O Lord,
An' I'm standin' in the need of prayer.

Ain't my mother or my father,
but it's me O Lord,
standin' in the need of prayer,
Ain't my mother or my father,
but it's me O Lord,
standin' in the need of prayer.

It's me, it's me O Lord,
standin' in the need of prayer,
It's me, It's me O Lord,
standin' in the need of prayer.

Not my deacon, not my leader,
but it's me O Lord,
standin' in the need of prayer,
Not my deacon, not my leader,
but it's me O Lord,
standin' in the need of prayer.

Were You There When They Crucified My Lord?

Were you there when they crucified my Lord?
Were you there,
were you there when they crucified by Lord?
Oh sometimes it causes me to trimble, trimble, trimble,
Were you there when they crucified my Lord?

Were you there when they nailed Him to the tree?
Were you there,
were you there when they nailed Him to the tree?
Oh sometimes it causes me to trimble, trimble, trimble,
Were you there when theynailed Him to the tree?

Were you there when they pierced him in the side?
Were you there,
were you there when they peirced him in the side?
Oh sometimes it causes me to trimble, trimble, trimble,
Were you there when they pierced him in the side?

Were you there when the sun refused to shine?
Were you there,
Were you there when the sun refused to shine?
Oh sometimes it causes me to trimble, trimble, trimble
Were you there when the sun rrefused to shine?

Were you there when they laid Him in the tomb?
Were you there,
were you there when they laid Him in the tomb?
Oh sometimes it causes me to trimble, trimble, trimble
Were you there when they laid Him in the tomb?

Wade In The Water

Wade in the water.
Wade in the water, children.
Wade in the water.
God's gonna trouble the water.

Well, who are these children all dressed in red?
God's a-gonna trouble the water
Must be the children that Moses led
God's a-gonna trouble the water.

Chorus

Who's that young girl dressed in white
Wade in the Water
Must be the Children of Israelites
God's gonna trouble the Water.

Chorus

Jordan's water is chilly and cold.
God's gonna trouble the water.
It chills the body, but not the soul.
God's gonna trouble the water.

Chorus

If you get there before I do.
God's gonna trouble the water.
Tell all of my friends I'm coming too.
God's gonna trouble the water.

Chorus

Every Time I Feel The Spirit

Ev'ry time I feel the Spirit moving in my heart I will pray.
Ev'ry time I feel the Spirit moving in my heart I will pray.

Upon the mountain when my Lord, spoke,
Out of his mouth came fire and smoke.
Look all around me, It looked so fine
'Til I asked my Lord if all were mine.

O, Every time I feel the spirit movein' in my heart, I will pray. Yes,
every time I feel the spirit movein' in my heart, I will pray.

Jordan river chilly and cold, chill my body but not my soul.
O, every time i feel the spirit movein' in my heart, i will pray.

Lift Every Voice And Sing

Lift every voice and sing, till earth and Heaven ring,
Ring with the harmonies of liberty;
Let our rejoicing rise, high as the listening skies,
Let it resound loud as the rolling sea.
Sing a song full of the faith that the dark past has taught us,
Sing a song full of the hope that the present has brought us;
Facing the rising sun of our new day begun,
Let us march on till victory is won.

Stony the road we trod, bitter the chastening rod,
Felt in the days when hope unborn had died;
Yet with a steady beat, have not our weary feet,
Come to the place for which our fathers sighed?
We have come over a way that with tears has been watered,
We have come, treading our path through the blood of the slaughtered;
Out from the gloomy past, till now we stand at last
Where the white gleam of our bright star is cast.

God of our weary years, God of our silent tears,
Thou Who hast brought us thus far on the way;
Thou Who hast by Thy might, led us into the light,
Keep us forever in the path, we pray.
Lest our feet stray from the places, our God, where we met Thee.
Lest our hearts, drunk with the wine of the world, we forget Thee.
Shadowed beneath Thy hand, may we forever stand,
True to our God, true to our native land.

Down By The Riverside

Gonna lay down my burden,
Down by the riverside,
Down by the riverside,
Down by the riverside.
Gonna lay down my burden,
Down by the riverside
To study war no more.

Chorus:
I ain't gonna study war no more;
Study war no more;
Study war no more.
I ain't gonna study war no more;
Study war no more;
Study war no more.